Dedicated to our inspiring friend
ROBERT E. SNODGRASS
who shared his creative nature.

Special thanks to the David and Lucile Packard Foundation.

Copyright © 2000 by Dawn Navarro
All rights reserved, Published by Sea Challengers in association with Manta Publications.

Dan Gotshall, Editorial Director
Dawn Navarro, Art Director-Book Designer-Illustrator
Wallace 'J' Nichols, Scientific Advisor-Writer
Roxane Buck-Ezcurra, Scientific Editor-Story Editor
Dominique Navarro, Book Editor
Robert Cuoto, Electronic Production Consultant
Wendy Ray, Book Production Associate
Ann Gotshall, Advertising-Publicist

No part of this publication may be reproduced in whole or in part, or stored in a retrieval system or transmitted in any form or by any means electronic, mechanical, photocopying, recording or otherwise without written permission of the publishers. For information regarding permission write Manta Publications, 30069 Harvester Road, Malibu, CA 90265.
Printed in Hong Kong through Global Interprint, Inc., San Francisco.

Library of Congress Cataloging-in-Publication Data
Navarro, Dawn.
Chelonia: return of the sea turtle
p. cm.
ISBN 0-930118-31-6
1. Green turtle--Mexico--Baja California (Peninsula)--Biography--Juvenile Literature.
2. Wildlife rescue--Mexico---Baja California (Peninsula)--Biography--Juvenile Literature.
[1. Green turtle. 2. Turtles. 3. Wildlife rescue.] I. Title.
QL666.C536 N28 2001
597.92--dc21
00-066172

Watch for the sea glossaries.

BASED ON A TRUE STORY

CHELONIA
Return of the Sea Turtle

DAWN E. NAVARRO
ROBERT E. SNODGRASS
WALLACE J. NICHOLS

MANTA PUBLICATIONS

SEA CHALLENGERS

It was midday in August 1971. An El Niño tropical storm was brewing to the south.

Nina Delmar and her father navigated their sturdy yacht on its homeward cruise off Mexico's coast. Wind-swept clouds darkened the sky above. Beneath, the deep waters churned and rolled.

They watched the sea with steady eyes as they faced the most difficult passage of their journey.

SEA LOG

Five hundred miles south of the U.S. border, in Baja California, Mexico, the sea is big and blue. Dolphins swim and play here. Sea turtles from Michoacán nesting beaches come to feed on crabs and sea grass. Giant whales feed on fish and krill. The cruise north off the Baja coast is infamous and appropriately named "the uphill passage" by seafarers. The name describes the climb boats must make to the top of each wave coming out of the north.

Bottlenose Dolphin
Tursiops truncatus

White-sided Dolphin
Lagenorhynchus obliquidens

Common Dolphin
Delphinus delphis

Nina's father felt the fury of the sea. "We can't beat this storm before dark," he shouted. "We'll have to ride it through the night."

"The dolphins are gone, Papa," Nina cried out over the howling wind.

An albatross grazed its wing on the crest of a wave rising before them. Rain clouds blocked the last rays of sunlight and the sea turned angry gray.

That night Nina hid in her tiny bunk below deck. She wished that she could dive deep below the waves like a dolphin, or fly away like a seagull.

SEA LOG

During storms, dolphins can dive beneath the waves to calm water. They return to the surface only to catch a breath of air. Birds often glide just above the waves using the rising crests for lift. Both dolphins and birds are adapted to survive in rough weather, but some storms are difficult in the open sea, especially for the young.
Only the strong and lucky survive.

Storm Petrel
Oceanodroma leucorhoa

Albatross
Diomedea albatrus

Seagull
Larus occidentalis

Through the night the storm's strong current swept a young sea turtle far out of its normal range. The little animal struggled hour after hour in the dark and chilling sea.

With the light of dawn the storm had passed. The weak and weary turtle bobbed on the surface, barely able to lift its head for a breath of air.

SEA LOG

Tunas, sharks and other fish of the open ocean can be found hanging out underneath floating objects. In their world there are few hiding places; these objects may offer them protection. They also follow warm water currents which extend especially far to the north during the warmer El Niño years.

By mid morning the sea had calmed. But the hapless little turtle still rolled in the smooth waves.

A hungry tiger shark, scavenging after the storm, swallowed anything and everything he found. He spotted the sea turtle and moved towards his prey. However, something disturbed his hunt. The shark quickly circled deeper as a rumbling noise grew louder.

Just then, the Delmar's yacht crested a wave.

SEA LOG

After a storm, drifting debris, seaweed rafts and unlucky or stranded sea creatures accumulate along the edges of currents. The ocean's scavengers follow these "green lines" looking for a meal. In this way, sharks and seagulls clean up after a storm.

Surf Grass
Phyllospadix spp.

Giant Kelp
Macrocystis pyrifera

From the bow of the boat Nina kept watch on the sea, entranced by the excitement in the water. Tunas darted among the leaping dolphins. Whales splashed and sprayed.

Ahead she spotted an unusual shape. It looked like a small turtle to her. It was!

"Papa, look! A sea turtle," she cried. "It's looks hurt... can we help it?"

Papa turned the boat toward the floating animal. "Take the helm, bring her about, full stop!" he shouted.

Nina took control of the boat as her father rushed to the stern, stripping off his shirt and leaping into the cold water.

Papa grasped the helpless turtle with both hands. Nina threw him a life ring and helped pull her father and the rescued sea turtle to the boat.

Papa shivered as he climbed aboard. The tiger shark passed below unnoticed.

Nina wrapped her shivering father and the cold turtle in warm, dry blankets.

"What can we do?" Nina asked as she held the fragile bundle. The turtle was so weak it could hardly move. Its eyes were barely open.

"It might not survive, Nina. Let's put the turtle in this wooden box and let it rest," her father said gently.

Nina watched over the turtle for hours. She kept its eyes moist using an eyedropper.

It was late afternoon when they neared the California coast.

SEA LOG

All around the world, wildlife rescue centers work to save injured or stranded animals. It is everyone's responsibility to rescue animals in need of help. Whenever a tagged animal is encountered, the local stranding or rescue center should be contacted. Trained veterinarians work with the animals to rehabilitate them and return them to the wild.

SEA GLOSSARY

El Niño: an unusually warm surface current flowing along the west coasts of North and South America
seafarers: people who travel or work at sea
range: the area in which an animal lives
debris: discarded natural materials and trash
scavenging: searching through debris for things to eat
prey: an animal that is hunted and killed for food

By late evening the Delmars' yacht entered San Diego Bay. They docked at the U.S. Customs office.

"We have something to show you," declared Mr. Delmar.

"After the storm we rescued this baby sea turtle," Nina shared.

The customs officer looked at the small, limp turtle in the wooden box. "It's a green turtle, 'Chelonia mydas.' What a shame. There aren't many left these days. It doesn't look like this one will survive," he commented as he wrote on his clipboard.

"Chelonia," Nina whispered. "Don't worry, I'll take care of you."

When Nina and her father arrived home they were exhausted. But Nina filled their bathtub with warm water. This was a safe place for the sea turtle to spend the night.

Nina instantly fell asleep in her own comfortable bed. All night she dreamed of the storm, the dolphins and the seabirds. She imagined the sea rolling around her as if she were still on the boat.

SEA LOG

Chelonia mydas (pronounced ki-'lō-nē-a mī-das) is the scientific name for the green sea turtle. The Pacific green sea turtle is found in coastal waters, bays, lagoons, estuaries and the open ocean. They migrate thousands of miles with the currents along the Pacific Ocean coasts from nesting to feeding grounds.

The next morning Chelonia was revived by the warm water and rest. She swam and splashed in the bathtub. Her eyes were wide open with curiosity about her strange new environment. She was hungry and tried to bite a rubber ducky.

Nina spoke to the sea turtle as she took her into the backyard. "You need more room and salt water and food. You're going to like our pond, Chelonia."

SEA LOG

Sea turtles swim using their flippers to pull themselves through the water. Both flippers are used at the same time, moving up and down, much like a bird flying. The rear flippers are used as rudders to steer and to move backward. Turtles can swim fast and dash away quickly to escape danger and predators or to chase their prey. During migrations, green turtles may swim more than 20 miles each day.

By-the-Wind Sailor Jellyfish
Velella velella

The Delmar's backyard saltwater pond was home to a small garibaldi, a few reef fish and three young green moray eels. It was a comfortable new world for the small sea turtle who swam around exploring the rocks and resting on the sandy bottom.

Nina fed the turtle bits of fish and handfuls of sea grass she had collected in the ocean. In the months that followed, the little sea turtle grew bigger and bigger and bigger.

SEA LOG

In the wild, green sea turtles eat mostly algae and sea grass. They occasionally eat sea pens, sponges and jellyfish. In captivity, sea turtles are fed fish and squid and may grow two or three times faster than in the wild.

Sea Pen
Ptilosarcus gurneyi

Red Algae
Gracilaria sjoestedtii

All of the sea animals were well fed and grew quickly in the backyard pond. Chelonia could barely turn around she had grown so fast.

In just two years Nina's small turtle had grown into a large wild animal.

"Chelonia, how big do green sea turtles grow?" Nina wondered, "And what are we to do about you? You need a bigger home."

5 years

20 years old

Hatchling

SEA LOG

When green turtle hatchlings are born, they are smaller than the palm of your hand. It can take a green turtle 5 years to reach the size of a small platter. It may take them more than 20 years to reach maturity (approximately 30 inches). Green turtles can grow to be more than a yard long (300 pounds) and may live for 100 years.

The Aquarium's marine biologist told Nina that she had done a great thing by saving Chelonia's life. He also explained to her that the 1973 Endangered Species Act now protects all sea turtles. "The next time you find an injured animal, please contact us right away. Chelonia is a female turtle. Returning her to the ocean will help her species survive," he said. "We'll watch her behavior, check her health and tag her before we release her into the ocean."

A few weeks later Nina was invited to help release the healthy, strong green turtle. They sailed out on a small boat into the Pacific Ocean. An underwater photographer documented Chelonia's release as the turtle quickly disappeared into the blue sea. "Vaya con dios, Chelonia." Nina waved goodbye.

Chelonia instinctively remembered everything about being a wild turtle. She swam south toward the warmer waters of Mexico eating jellyfish carried by the currents. While following the path of her ancestors, she avoided fishing nets that often drown sea turtles. Chelonia headed for the protected beach where she was born in Michoacán, Mexico. Green turtles have nested there for millions of years.

SEA LOG

Sea turtles thrive on jellyfish. But they often can't see the difference between drifting plastic bags and their jellyfish prey. When a sea turtle swallows plastic debris it will often cause the turtle to suffocate and die.

SEA GLOSSARY

garibaldi: a bright-orange marine fish
endangered: may become extinct
extinct: the death of an entire species
species: a group of closely related plants or animals
"Vaya con Dios": Farewell, God be with you.
instinctively: non-taught knowledge from birth; action without thought
ancestors: historical relatives; ancient family

Chelonia traveled for many months and swam thousands of miles in the ocean. She finally arrived at the beach where she was born. Hundreds of sea turtles gathered in the shallow waters. There were female and male turtles, brothers and sisters, cousin and nephew turtles. There were even aunts and uncles. Some of the turtles were 100 years old. All of the sea turtles came for the same reason—to mate and lay eggs.

SEA LOG

Adult male and female sea turtles can easily be distinguished. The males have long tails and big, curved claws. However, when the turtles are young it is difficult to tell the males from the females.

Female　　**Male**

One moonlit night, when the time was right, Chelonia moved through the waves and dragged herself up the sandy beach. She dug a deep pit with her rear flippers. Then she dropped one hundred perfectly round white eggs into her sandy nest. She carefully covered the eggs and returned to the sea.

Eight weeks later, on another moonlit night, Chelonia's eggs began to hatch. Baby sea turtles pulled themselves up through the sand and scrambled down the beach into the sea.

SEA LOG

Baby sea turtles are called hatchlings. Once hatched it takes the babies three days to climb through the sand out of the nest. They are able to locate the sea at night by moving toward the moonlit water. However, if there are bright lights from parking lots, roads or houses they will become confused and never find the ocean.

Many obstacles awaited as they made their journey to the ocean. Predators, such as crabs and raccoons, ambushed the hatchlings. Flocks of hungry seagulls hovered above, eyeing the turtles as an early morning meal.

Even in the water the surviving sea turtles were still not safe. They'd have to avoid the attacks of fish and sharks as well.

SEA LOG

From the hundreds of sea turtles that leave the nest only 10 percent will survive the first year of life. The dangers begin even before they hatch. Turtle eggs are savored as meals by predators including dogs, coyotes, foxes and seabirds. However, humans are the turtle's greatest predator. People dig up egg from nests and eat turtle meat despite the 1973 Endangered Species Act. The fate of the sea turtle lies in our hands. Will we give them the opportunity to live another hundred million years?

One little sea turtle would endure. And that turtle would return to this same beach someday to lay her eggs…

...just like Chelonia.

Sea turtles are endangered and disappearing from our oceans. You can help them survive by taking Nina's Sea Turtle Pledge and by supporting conservation groups working to rescue sea turtles and other marine animals.

My Sea Turtle Pledge

1. **Help Our Wildlife!** Call a professional wildlife rescue team when an animal needs rescuing.
2. **Respect wild animals.** Give them plenty of room on the beaches and in the ocean.
3. **Keep our beaches clean.**
4. **Keep our water clean.** No plastics and other trash in our oceans and streams.
5. **Ask Mama and Papa to buy only "Turtle Safe" seafood.**
6. **Learn more about the wild ocean animals** and tell your friends about sea turtles.

Nina Delmar

WILDCOAST
www.wildocean.com 619-423-8530

Alaska SeaLife Center
www.alaskasealife.org 907-224-6395

Seattle Aquarium
www.seattleaquarium.org 206-386-4330

Oregon Coast Aquarium
www.aquarium.org 541-867-3474

The Marine Mammal Center
www.tmmc.org Rescue Line 415-289-7325

Monterey Bay Aquarium
www.montereybayaquarium.org 831-648-4888

Aquarium of the Pacific
Long Beach, CA 90802
www.aquariumofpacific.org 562-590-3100

SeaWorld, San Diego
www.seaworld.org 619-222-6363

Sea Turtle Conservation Network of the Californias
www.baja-tortugas.org

Centro Mexicano de la Tortuga
cmtvasco@angel.umar.mx 958-43055

Mazatlan Aquarium
52-69-817815
acuario@pacificpearl.com

Costa Rica Sea Turtle Restoration Project
www.seaturtles.org
1203-1100

Central America Sea Turtle Conservation Network
560-2243570
Tortugas@sol.racsa.co.cr

WALLACE J. NICHOLS PH.D.

Wallace "J" Nichols has devoted himself to the study and conservation of sea turtles and working with the people who most greatly threaten the survival of the sea turtle species. He co-founded *WILDCOAST*, a non-profit organization dedicated to marine conservation and education. J studied Wildlife Ecology at the University of Arizona, holds a Master's degree in Natural Resource Economics and Policy from Duke University School of Environment, and a Bachelor's degree in Biology and Spanish from DePauw University. His studies in the marine environment have taken him from South America to the Arctic Circle. As a Fulbright Fellow he focused his research on the trans-Pacific migration of the loggerhead turtle from Baja California to Japan. Working closely with fishermen they are learning about turtle behavior and easing exploitation pressure on endangered populations. This research project has reached hundreds of thousands of school children around the world through articles published in National Geographic magazines and the web page www.wildocean.com.
For many years J collected turtle poetry and stories knowing that storytelling is creative and effective education.
J met Robert Snodgrass while releasing a sea turtle in Baja. Working together, they shared optimistic messages about the survival of the sea turtle.

ROBERT E. SNODGRASS

Robert Snodgrass was dedicated to the study of natural ocean history and marine biology. At the age of sixteen he became an active junior volunteer at UCSD's Scripps Institution of Oceanography in La Jolla, California. After graduation from U.C. Berkeley he returned to the Scripps Aquarium to become the Curator of Collections and Fish. An international aquarium consultant, he specialized in aquarium design and marine life support systems as well as animal husbandry and a technique of creating fish community tanks. Robert was an experienced diver who was as comfortable as a fish "underwater" and documented his experiences with videotape.
As a naturalist he gave lectures, classes and guided natural history tours, dives and walks in the La Jolla cove for more than two decades. He also led collection expeditions and trips to the Sea of Cortez. Robert was an accomplished writer who wrote a *Los Angeles Times* syndicated newspaper column "OCEAN ENCOUNTER" for five years. He dreamed of "sharing his knowledge," experiences and stories beyond the dozens of educational books and papers produced for the aquarium. His life goal was to bring to the people who might never "experience it firsthand" the fragile and increasingly endangered ecosystem of the sea.

DAWN E. NAVARRO

Dawn Navarro studied illustration and design at the Art Center College of Design, Los Angeles. After graduation she worked as an art director and freelance designer for such companies as Walt Disney, Needham, Harper & Steers Advertising and the Los Angeles Times. As an naturalist artist, she focuses her interests in marine and terrestrial ecology. During a diving and fish collecting expedition to the Sea of Cortez, Dawn met Robert Snodgrass. This was the beginning of the black and white naturalistic studies and animal behavior illustrations that became the visual art for the newspaper column "OCEAN ENCOUNTER." Together, Robert Snodgrass and Dawn teamed as MANTA Publications to produce marine and natural history posters and books.